CHOOSE JUSTICE

BY MARIBEL VALDEZ GONZALEZ

CAPSTONE PRESS

a capstone imprint

Published by Capstone Press, an imprint of Capstone
1710 Roe Crest Drive, North Mankato, Minnesota 56003
capstonepub.com

Library of Congress Cataloging-in-Publication Data is available on the Library of Congress
website.
ISBN: 9781666345476 (hardcover)
ISBN: 9781666345490 (paperback)
ISBN: 9781666345506 (ebook PDF)

Summary: How do you know that something is unfair? What can you do about it? Learn about
ways to recognize injustice, examples of injustice in the past, and how you can help work
toward justice.

Editorial Credits
Editor: Ericka Smith; Designer: Sarah Bennett; Media Researcher: Svetlana Zhurkin;
Production Specialist: Katy LaVigne

Image Credits
Alamy: David Grossman, 26, Everett Collection Inc, 22, Xinhua/Bao Dandan, 13; Getty
Images: Chip Somodevilla, 15, Jose Luis Pelaez Inc, 28, Star Tribune/Pete Hohn, 12;
Shutterstock Premier: The LIFE Picture Collection/Loomis Dean, 11; Shutterstock:
arindambanerjee, 24, Avava, 7, bgrocker, 6, Everett Collection, 9, Jelani Photography, 4, Joseph
Gruber, 19, Kathy Hutchins, 23, Kite_rin, 27, Linda Parton, 14, Magnia (background), back
cover and throughout, Monkey Business Images, 17, Phil Pasquini, 21, PR Image Factory, 16,
Receh Lancar Jaya, cover, Rob Crandall, 29, Sheila Fitzgerald, 18, Zac Hancock, 5

TABLE OF CONTENTS

Words in **bold** are in the glossary.

WHY CHOOSE JUSTICE?

We all want to live in a world that is fair. But not everyone is treated fairly. People often treat others unfairly because of things like their race, gender, or sexual identity. They might also be treated unfairly because of their religion, abilities, or class.

FACT Our race, gender, sexual identity, religion, class, and abilities are called social identities. They're how we are grouped with other people.

How can we help make things fair? First, we must be able to recognize injustice. This means we understand how people and organizations treat others unfairly and cause harm. Then we can think of ways to bring about justice—or get rid of unfairness and harm. And we must act.

Working toward justice is hard. But each one of us can do this work. We can do it alone. And we can do it with others. We can help create a world where everyone is treated fairly and can live freely.

CHAPTER 1

WHAT IS INJUSTICE?

Injustice is when people do something that is unfair or wrong. What if a teacher only told some students about an upcoming test? Not everyone would have the same chance of doing well. That would be unfair.

People often do things that are unfair because they have a **bias** against another group. That means they favor others over that group. Often people favor the groups they belong to.

STEREOTYPING

Sometimes we make assumptions about others because they belong to a certain group. We call those stereotypes. One stereotype is that girls are not good at math. Stereotypes can be a part of the reason we hold a bias against another group. And that can impact how we treat one another. For example, maybe a math teacher does not call on girls as often as they call on boys to answer questions.

Sometimes we can see this in the way people interact with one another. Maybe a white cashier at a store is rude to Black customers, but friendly with white customers.

But we also often see bias in the ways that organizations treat certain groups. One way we see this is in our rules or laws. In the United States, there was a time when only white men who owned land could vote. Those laws were unfair to people of color, women, and people with less money.

Looking at history can show us patterns of bias. Seeing the pattern makes it easier to see injustice in our own communities and helps us work toward justice.

A woman votes in a 1920 election after the Nineteenth Amendment gave women in the U.S. the legal right to vote.

TREATMENT OF LATINE MIGRANTS

In 2017 and 2018, **migrant** families from Mexico and Central American countries were harmed by the U.S. government. When they came to the U.S. without permission from the government to pursue a different life, parents were separated from their children. They were separated so that the parents could be charged with breaking the law.

Their children were held in buildings with poor living conditions. And the government did not have a good plan for getting them back to their families. Separating **Latine** families showed that the U.S. government did not respect their rights as humans.

 FACT During World War II, the U.S. didn't have enough farmworkers. From 1942 to 1964, millions of Mexican workers came to the U.S. to work under the Bracero Program, an agreement between the two countries.

Latine migrants were forced to leave the U.S. in the 1950s.

This is part of a pattern of poor treatment of Latine migrants in the U.S. In the 1950s, many migrants were **deported** to Mexico. They had come to the U.S. to work. Some had permission and others did not. And some were citizens of the U.S. They were deported because some people feared they would take jobs from other Americans.

BANNING SAME-SEX MARRIAGE

To get married, couples have to apply for a license in their state. In the 1970s, states began to ban same-sex marriages, so same-sex couples couldn't get a license to get married. This was happening at the same time that the gay rights movement was starting.

Some people held religious beliefs that did not support same-sex relationships. Some people feared changes to their ideas about marriage and family.

THE FIRST SUPREME COURT CASE ON SAME-SEX MARRIAGE

In 1970, Jack Baker and Michael McConnell tried to get a marriage license in Minnesota. At the time, Minnesota's laws didn't say only men and women could marry, but they were denied anyway. Their case went all the way to the Supreme Court, but the court would not review the case. That decision made it possible for states to ban same-sex marriages without the federal government trying to stop them.

In 1996, the federal government passed a law that protected those bans. More and more states began banning same-sex marriages.

Without being married, some same-sex couples could not do a lot of important things. Getting medical care for their partners wasn't always allowed. Adopting a child was difficult.

It wasn't until 2003 that Massachusetts became the first state to make same-sex marriage legal. In 2015, the U.S. Supreme Court made a decision that required all states to accept marriages between same-sex couples.

CONTAMINATED WATER IN MICHIGAN

In 2014, the city of Flint, Michigan, tried to save money on its drinking water. They decided to get drinking water from the Flint River. Poor testing and treatment of the water led to serious health issues for people. The water caused hair loss, skin rashes, and other problems.

Not having clean drinking water is an injustice. The problem in Flint is rooted in **racism** and **classism**. About 54 percent of the people who live in the city are Black. About 40 percent of the residents experience poverty. Officials knew of the problem but were slow to respond. This showed that they didn't care as much about the needs of Black people and people experiencing poverty.

Residents held meetings. They sent **petitions** to the Environmental Protection Agency. And they filed lawsuits against the city of Flint.

The residents' actions have helped bring attention to the issue. They are making progress toward getting clean water.

CHAPTER 2

WHAT IS JUSTICE?

Once we can see injustice, then we have to think about how to change it. What is justice? Justice is when laws, rules, and practices are fair. Justice means we are taking steps toward making sure everyone can live freely.

People have different ideas about what justice looks like. What do you think it looks like? Consider these questions:

- What does each family have?
- What kinds of jobs do people have?
- How are kids treated at school?
- How are adults treated at work?
- How do people treat each other in their community?
- What things can people do in their neighborhood?

Once we can imagine a world with justice, how do we work toward it? What does it take to see justice in our communities? Think about these questions:

- What laws need to change?
- What rules need to change?
- What behaviors need to change?
- Who can help make those changes?
- What might make it hard to create that change?

Students participate in a lie-in outside the White House in 2018 to call for stronger gun control laws.

FACT In 2016, middle schooler Kristen Wong received a warning for wearing a tank top—a violation of the school's dress code. Wong found out that girls were punished more often than boys for violating the dress code. She worked with teachers and students to change her school's dress code—and later the entire district's dress code in Alameda, California.

CHAPTER 3

TAKING ACTION TO ACHIEVE JUSTICE

Now that we have an idea of a world with justice and how we might achieve it, let's think about the actions we can each take to get there. We can help achieve justice by:

- taking action against injustices that we see or experience.
- supporting other people who are treated unfairly because of their identities.

It's important to do both to help achieve justice. It helps us see how different forms of injustice are connected. And that helps us think about what's best for everyone—not just ourselves.

TAKING ACTION

People work to address injustice in different ways. Their actions help bring about important changes in our world. Here are two examples:

➡ In 1957, three years after *Brown v. Board of Education* outlawed **segregation** in schools, a group of nine Black students was the first to attend an all-white high school in Little Rock, Arkansas. The group is called the Little Rock Nine. They were **harassed** by white students and adults, and the National Guard had to protect them. It was a very hard year for the students. But they started the process of integrating schools in Little Rock.

The National Guard protects the Little Rock Nine as they walk to school.

➡ In 2015, Xiuhtezcatl Martinez, an **Indigenous** activist, joined a lawsuit against the U.S. government. Martinez and a group of students sued the government for failing to address climate change. They were worried about the effects problems like flooding and droughts—brought on by climate change—might have on their lives.

Xiuhtezcatl Martinez

The Little Rock Nine and Martinez took action to help address injustice in their communities. What are some ways people might take action based on these examples?

ACTING IN SOLIDARITY

Solidarity is action you can take to support people being treated unfairly. This can be making sure people know about an issue. Or it can be using your privilege to help someone. Solidarity is supporting others without asking for anything in return.

Protesters showing solidarity with Indigenous people who fought against the construction of the Dakota Access Pipeline.

IDEAS IN ACTION

During a discussion about Thanksgiving, the teacher, Ms. Johnson, shared that the Plymouth pilgrims invited the Wampanoag people to a feast to give thanks for their survival in 1621.

Aneesha, an Indian American student, knew this story was not correct. She raised her hand. Ms. Johnson called on her.

"This version of the story doesn't tell the truth about the experience of the Wampanoag. It doesn't talk about violence toward Indigenous people and their deaths from the colonists' diseases," Aneesha said. "I think it's important that we discuss the truth."

Aneesha's class has community agreements—guidelines the group has created for interacting with one another. One of the community agreements in Aneesha's class is to talk about things that are uncomfortable. This means that students and the teacher know that in order to address unfairness, they must have challenging conversations.

Ms. Johnson said to Aneesha, "Okay, tell me more. I'm willing to learn from you."

Who was Aneesha showing solidarity with?

We can act in solidarity by using our privilege. Everyone has privilege. Privilege is an unearned benefit someone has just because they belong to a certain group. For example, someone might have privilege because they are white, a man, or nondisabled.

When people are treated unfairly, it can sometimes be difficult to talk about. So sometimes it's helpful when a person with privilege uses their voice to help inform people and bring about change. But we should make sure we're not speaking over people who are treated unfairly.

IDEAS IN ACTION

Safiya is a Black girl from a wealthy family. Safiya's best friend is Katie. Katie is a white girl from a working-class family.

When kids at their school made fun of Katie for having older sneakers, Safiya spoke up and said, "It's not nice to make fun of what people wear. Besides, why does it matter what sort of shoes Katie has?"

When kids at their school teased Safiya about her hair, Katie spoke up and said, "Why would you say that? There's nothing wrong with Safiya's hair because it's different from yours."

How are Katie and Safiya acting in solidarity with each other?

Choosing justice means choosing a future where we are all free. First, we must be able to identify injustice. Next, we need to imagine what justice for all people can look like. Then, we can work with others to transform our communities.

What we do to bring about justice will look different for everyone. We have different identities, experiences, and privilege. All of it can help us as we seek justice and move toward freedom.

GLOSSARY

bias (BYE-uhs)—favoring one group over another

classism (KLASS-iz-uhm)—negative attitudes toward people with less money or education

deport (di-PORT)—to send people back to the country they came from

harass (huh-RASS)—to bother or annoy again and again

Indigenous (in-DIJ-uh-nuss)—belonging to the group of people who first lived in a place

Latine (la-TEE-neh)—from or having ancestors from a country in Latin America, such as the Dominican Republic, Mexico, or Chile

migrant (MY-gruhnt)—a person who moves to a new area or country, usually in search of work

petition (puh-TISH-uhn)—a letter signed by many people asking leaders for a change

racism (RAY-siz-uhm)—the belief that one race is better than another race

segregation (seg-ruh-GAY-shuhn)—the practice of keeping groups of people apart, especially based on race

READ MORE

Garcia, Laleña. *What We Believe: A Black Lives Matter Principles Activity Book*. New York: Lee & Low, 2020.

Harris, Duchess, and Tammy Gagne. *Justice for George Floyd*. Minneapolis: Abdo Publishing, 2021.

Rebel Girls. *Rebel Girls Lead: 25 Tales of Powerful Women*. Los Angeles: Rebel Girls, Inc., 2020.

INTERNET SITES

Do Something
dosomething.org/us

Roots & Shoots United States
rootsandshoots.org

Young Voices for the Planet
youngvoicesfortheplanet.com/for-kids/

INDEX

ABOUT THE AUTHOR

Maribel Valdez Gonzalez is an Indigenous Xicana STEM/PBL coach, former classroom teacher, and consultant. She resides in occupied Duwamish territory, also known as Seattle, Washington. She is from occupied Somi Se'k land, also known as San Antonio, Texas. In her 10 years as an antiracist educator, Maribel has been honored to work with youth and adults to decolonize and humanize teaching practices and belief systems in classrooms and beyond. Maribel's goal is to create academically engaging learning experiences through a culturally sustaining environment that fosters empowerment, healing, and radical kindness. She is also a member of the Antiracist Arts Education Task Force for Visual & Performing Arts in Seattle Public Schools.